Searching for Clarity

SEARCHING

FOR

CLARITY

Poems

GENE ZIMMERMAN

Published in the United States of America

Snow Capped Consulting, LLC.

Gene Zimmerman
Snow Capped Consulting, LLC.
1623 S.E. Malden St.
Portland, Oregon 97202
(503) 985-9750
info@snowcappedconsulting.com

ISBN: 978-1-7370124-0-5 (paperback)
ISBN: 978-1-7370124-1-2 (ebook)

Cover photograph © Krystof Guth / Shutterstock

Cover and text design by Pratt Brothers Composition

In memory of
Claire Miller Zimmerman
1955–2015

So deeply thankful for the love
and all we shared in our time together,
and for our two beautiful children,
Chloe and Eric.

Contents

Preface

Poetry came to me during the most challenging time of my life. When my wife, Claire, struggled with an illness that ultimately took her life, I was immensely moved to put my thoughts and feelings on paper. I've continued to write and study poetry ever since.

When life brings hardships and massive challenges, it's hard to get through what needs to be done or even determine what needs to be done. No playbook is issued. It can be the loneliest of experiences, regardless of how many people are around. At such times, it's difficult to understand yourself and what's happening, much less explain it to others.

This collection, written during those years of hardship, is offered to those who find themselves in a life-altering situation not experienced by most. My hope is that the following poems may give some relief simply by sharing the immense grief, loss, stress, financial devastation, and overwhelming feelings that can be experienced when being with a critically sick or challenged loved one.

Searching for Clarity

The View

I like that view,
The reds and yellows
Have invaded the leaves,
Pushed by the breezes, they wave.

The arm of the bay
Separates the land,
The water smooth and flowing,
Both sides inviting.

A stroll through the trees
Following the water
Sets the mind at ease,
Why doesn't this happen more often?

As birds fly overhead
The bench is patient,
Though not always chosen.
It holds its stories.

Sentinels

They stand by the water's edge,
Some tall, some short,
Some wide, some skinny,
Their heads all unique.

Distinctive yet the same,
Enduring and peaceful,
Shaped by time or hand
These timbers.

Leftover from a long-gone era
Or placed by an artist
It matters not,
The vigil is the same.

Presence through light and dark
Alters the landscape.
Perceptions are changed,
Is this you?

The Nest

A window gives a view,
The sun shines on leaves,
Birds flit about,
Sometimes one, sometimes more.

Playing in a small wooded sanctuary,
Food and water all around,
A brilliant blue sky,
The birds are soaring, always soaring.

Is there trouble in the nest?
Do daily problems keep rising?
Will the squirrels take the food?
How does the day move forward?

Everything looks to be in order,
Surely there can be no strife
In a life that appears to have it all,
If only that were so.

The Dungeon

The thought is pushed away,
No, not today.
When will I open up?
And examine further.

The stone steps
Lead deep into the dungeon,
Torches in their holders
Darkness gets bolder and bolder.

Sometimes skimming the surface,
Other times, diving its deepest
Crushing, numbing, is the fear
Of not knowing,
Not being able to move.

The day is too precious
To let slip away
With another wrestle,
That leads no way.

Searching

Loss happens, teeth clench,
What was to be,
Swept away never being more
Than the thought it was.

For now, the days drift
Uncertain and mostly cloudy
Searching, searching for a point,
To drop anchor, in a harbor that's safe.

No one can see
From one moment to the next,
Yet surely, there is a path
That can be followed.

Stumble, then stumble again
Eyes closed
Mind racing
Heart pounding

Togetherness

Togetherness, what comfort.
Wrapped in a cocoon,
Nothing intrudes
But sweet solitude.

Closeness that can't be measured,
Two souls communing,
Drifting, drifting gently through the day.
All judgments suspended.

The warmth, the touch,
Intimate but lazy,
Like a river kissed by the sun
Starts from here and goes to there.

Surrendering as long as possible,
Maybe the entire day,
It won't always be like this.
For now, love and bliss.

Let It Go

There was no choice,
But to let it all go.
Like a ghostly apparition
In bright light.

The hard line
Of struggle and survival,
Inserted itself, most unwelcome
Though it may be.

No past, no future,
Only now and how to live,
Continuously,
Day after day.

What was taken from me
And those closest around,
With no idea of how long,
Possibly never to be gained back.

Angry

How can I not be angry?
Taken from me so completely
That which I love so dearly,
The hole so deep, only gets deeper.

My life was issued a stop,
A massive crash,
Sure to end the line
Of what had been nurtured.

Time together now and forever,
Has been shortened to now,
Left with so little,
But longing for it all.

Oh God really,
Is this a plan?
To inject such suffering and bad fate
Upon this very fragile plate.

It Mattered

Now as I sit and breathe,
The strongest feeling is to grieve,
Stress given off in waves,
Struggling to be brave.

How to continue, how to go on?
This isn't like caring for a lawn
Where water and nutrients
Are all that one needs.

The great anchor has been thrown out,
And now we are held in place,
Very little room to move,
Life is at a very different pace.

What used to be known,
As far as direction, commitment and striving,
Is now reduced and tattered,
It once so greatly mattered.

Not Now

It breaks my heart,
Day after day,
To see all you once had,
Taken away.

What can I offer?
What can I do?
But offer to you,
Time together, just you and me.

The days became weeks,
The weeks became months,
The months became years,
How much time left, is still unknown.

Our vows said, "in sickness and in health,"
We have known both.
"Till death do us part,"
Not now, how can it be?

Golden Age

It was a golden age,
Magic was in the air,
The children ran and laughed,
Played many games and yelled, "That's not fair."

For a time,
We were all blessed with health.
The hallways had chases
And were found many hiding spaces.

The dogs very spirited would join in,
Let loose their bark,
For all to hear,
It's exciting, come now.

Fond to look back,
Remembering that time,
It dances in the mind,
Swirling and twirling with great ease.

Pressure

The volcanic pressure grips,
There is going to be no diamond
Formed from this coal.
Wrong material, unfortunately, it's me.

I can't take another breath.
My mind screams,
There is no answer to any of this,
I have entered a complete abyss.

The choice is to let go.
Let go of it all.
Even more terrifying,
There is no choice.

How can any of it survive?
Why is it so complicated?
I've been ripped from my whole life,
I don't know why.

Glow

My eyes drop on something
And my heart falls to my feet.
It has her glow attached to it,
Her laugh, her smile, her eyes.

It brings memories long forgotten
To the surface, like it was yesterday.
They play in the air,
Leaving me often sad and empty.

The union that used to exist
Slowly slips away,
I don't want it to,
Some life is left.

Time has stopped.
There is a void,
Nothing can move,
This isn't that time.

Sick

To tell the truth,
It all makes me sick.
My stomach aches.
My nerves are shot.

If my death came now,
What a welcome relief,
As long as it's swift,
Not agonizing and lingering.

Why would I care?
Over there is over there.
Will I know or does knowing stop?
Hell is already with me.

As the stress burns like fire,
Constant, continuous, always,
What makes me move on?
Hope for a phoenix arising.

Taken

The face I see,
Is not the one from the picture.
What we talk about,
Doesn't have the depth.

You have been taken,
Not just from me,
But from yourself and others.
What do the children think?

There is no guide or handbook,
We all do the best we can.
Never knowing, is it enough?
But trying and caring continues.

Until the journey in life's canoe
Comes to an end.
Then we say goodbye,
To Daughter, Granddaughter, Sister,
    Niece, Cousin, Friend,
Wife and Mother.

Silence

This silence is welcome.
It's comfortable, peaceful, serene,
The days aren't all like this,
How wonderful to be calm.

Things will change.
Now is so tranquil.
Just being with each other,
Time where it's all relaxed.

It's grey outside.
It feels grey inside.
Time has stalled,
For now, it's just time to be.

Which has now become,
The best for which to hope.
Time precious time,
How much we have is unknown.

Slept

The grass heads were at season's end,
The tips plump and long,
Swaying in the wind,
Gently moving through the day.

The sun lit the trees, rocks and plants.
I looked on as you slept,
So much better than the days I've wept.
You've had it all taken away.

I'm here to give
What I can at this time.
It seems so much, it seems so little,
All with unknown time.

As I lift to go,
Your eyes open and search
For a time long ago,
When everything was all right.

Cliff

I've slipped and fallen.
With no strength to get back up,
Hanging onto the face of this cliff
With nothing but a tenacious grip.

Letting go will be terrifying.
No idea how far I will fall.
Grip and grip and grip
Just a little more time.

Will I slip with nothing left?
If so, can it be any worse
Than the path that lead to this cliff?
Nothing is known about after this.

It all seems to go black,
When a twist appears,
Another day is on the horizon.
I can make it one more day.

Being with You

I want to be in that place,
Where just being with you,
Is all that matters in the world.
It seems so real.

I can find it in my mind,
It fires my soul.
Yearning comes to join,
My breathing skips, my heart beats faster.

Being mine and intertwined
Was heaven I didn't know,
Until we came together.
Now that place burns so real.

As I reach and try to hold it longer
Its power still reverberates,
I'll be back
Because I never want to leave.

Well of Tears

I've hit the well of tears.
Just a minute ago
I had no idea where it was,
As they stream down my face

I've come to understand
What a strong and powerful thing
Each breach brings.
Trying neither to summon or ignore.

I find it with me
Most of the time hidden,
Not something easily pulled out.
Pressure blowing out like a geyser.

Feeling the pain bottled away
And the healing of relief,
Simultaneously, I move on.
The Well of Tears runs deep.

You Knew

I don't suppose you will ever know,
How deep and far I've fallen.
There was no asking or telling
But you knew I wasn't quite right.

As the weeks, months and years mounted
Your constant presence and concern counted.
Days where I wasn't together or connected
You gave precious relief and introspection.

So much continual confusion and complexity,
It just won't stop, it keeps getting worse.
Worn to the point of ragged,
Nerves are worked until completely broken.

Staggering through the days, stumbling and falling.
My biggest job was to get up, to face another day.
Made much more possible,
By your kindness and caring.

Life's Boat

Falling out of life's boat,
The water parted when the splash happened.
Downward, the sinking began,
Slowly, drifting deeper and deeper.

It felt like being a drowning victim.
Silence and the depths continued to rise,
Gentle rocking, like in a cradle,
Eyes wide open, lips not moving.

Struggling didn't help in the least.
I couldn't get any air,
How far is it to there?
How long will this continue?

The point was passed
Where it seemed unlikely
That the ability to rise would ever happen.
This far down, who would know?

Struggle

When someone young dies,
It's said, what a shame.
They should have had more time,
As if it's on a scale.

When someone old dies,
It's said, what a blessing.
It was a good long life.
Good isn't granted to everyone.

Somewhere between birth and death
Is a period of awful struggle,
The body is breaking down and usually
Requiring a significant financial commitment.

Lives are lost trying to help,
Not of this earth but of themselves.
The sufferer is just that,
All of it's taken, sometimes really slowly.

Hospital Time

It started as gleaming palaces
Where you are saved.
Everything here is so up to date,
Problems found will be fixed.

As the problems grew more complex,
Hospital time grew and grew.
In hours, days and weeks
The top-drawer look began to fade.

Not knowing and continual tests
Came wave after wave.
This wasn't simple it was really complex,
So time is spent in wandering,

Through the halls, waiting rooms,
    cafeteria and chapel.
Looking for any relief, a way to process
What is becoming life's routine and now makes
    something
I can barely stand, Hospital Time.

Death's Door

One day as I strode by,
Death's dark door cracked open.
I didn't like what I saw or felt,
For now in my life, it dwelt.

Wait, this can't be!
She will get better, you'll see.
If only this were in the cards,
Once the door opens, the tracking begins.

Not that it came often
But visits were made.
Invitations to visit the door,
Hard to put off and ignore.

As hope begins to sink,
There is no way but to realize,
Life will never again get to be,
A happy long living reality.

Can't Go Home

I walk along in the dark of night,
Wondering what you are thinking of.
Knowing you are safe and warm is a help.
How can it not be so very lonely?

When it was said, your wife's illness
    won't allow her to go home,
Not only was I in shock,
But had to deliver to you the message.
How do you say, you aren't coming home?

Oh God, I don't want to do this.
While knowing inside, this is all way past me.
Of all the talks we've ever had,
This one had to be the most sad.

So I visit most every day,
Still never seems enough.
We talk and share what time
There is still left together.

Tears

Thought I was through it.
The jarring emotion and significant outpouring
Had passed and was now gone.
Turns out, I was wrong.

Doesn't matter if there has been any preparation,
It hits from one instance to the next.
As deep and strong as ever,
I can't hold it back.

Where is this place
That it's from?
I search my thoughts and feelings,
Nothing is reveled, it's not working.

Yet there it goes,
I've resigned myself to let it.
So whoever I'm in front of,
Will just have to see how tears flow.

Safety Rope

When I was pushed into life's lake,
You threw the safety rope that trailed.
It gave me something to grab onto,
As I was dragged, twisting and turning

Like a person learning how to water-ski.
Holding on tight just being pulled,
No chance to get up.
I tried and tried.

If that safety rope hadn't been there,
I don't want to think about the added despair.
I was incapable of self-movement,
Drifting and vacant.

Your gift keeps giving,
For that I will be eternally grateful.
The cause, change and effect
Kept me moving.

Special Place

I usually have to push
To get myself through the day.
Not today, it's flowing without minute-to-minute
   pressing cares.
At the moment of notice it feels good.

There can always be found,
Ten to fifteen things to do,
Provided I wanted to see an output increase.
Slow down, pull back, it's really ok to
   let my guard down.

Sometimes and often for long periods
I hold on with a tenacious grip.
Each and every day
Looking for what needs to be done,
   avoiding penalty.

It's really a special place,
Not having to worry about impending doom
Every second of every day.
For today, I will give myself another hour.

Did He Die

Of course this happened!
Knew it would all along.
This friend of mine,
Of many years and great laughs.

So many stories and much history,
Gone without a trace.
Cell doesn't work, no text response,
All email accounts don't reply.

The only option left is snail mail.
Is he sick? Did he die?
Is he paralyzed? Is there a brain trauma?
Nothing is known, still a little hope.

He qualifies as one of the world's great recluses.
A very private world,
Hard to understand, harder to penetrate.
Missing you, my great friend.

Shut Off

I got the call.
Turns out, I wasn't just on ignore.
Something bad had happened to you,
A car wreck takes seconds.

What happened to you, became forever.
How can such damage occur so fast?
To have movement, thought and being,
Reduced to nothing more than suffering in a bed.

Locked inside, not being able to speak.
No chance of eating,
Without that tube in your stomach.
Everything shut off or broken.

We don't want you to go!
We love you so much,
Your time is now, your suffering will end.
If only life didn't go away.

Unplugged

I know it's the right thing.
Discussions were had,
Experts all weighed in.
It's all so devastating,
Created by a car crash.

Most of you was already shut down.
To keep the hell going
That you were existing in,
Would be an un-pardoning act.
The machines were unplugged.

As soon as the information was shared
I had an instant and sharp longing
For one more good laugh.
Another crazy story from the newspaper to share,
To talk as we've always done.

Now you are gone.
Grief, heavy and real.
Unlimited time will be spent thinking about
The memories of you.

So Long

The November skies are grey and vacant,
All the plants on the patio have died.
We are sitting in silence,
Sharing time and place.

After all the horrific circumstances
We have been through,
Today's are pale by comparison.
Thankful for that.

It's so hard to keep going
When there is never a time of knowing,
What is going to happen and when.
Just started year number five.

How can it be so long,
This major chunk out of all our lives.
How much more?
We will continue to take, one day at a time.

Sister

A visit from your sister
Will be happening shortly.
Good news for you and me.
A welcome connection for you, a breather for me.

I'm thankful for all visits.
It gives me some time
To do things that normally can't be done,
Also to grieve.

The visits have deep meaning
Because this may be the last one.
Bedside is now the only way,
The field trips, restaurants and shopping
    are long gone.

It's hard to make time in your schedule,
Especially when you live on the other coast.
But when you enter that door,
The loving, caring and sharing are truly priceless.

Here Now

There are times,
When I'm thinking of somebody
No longer with us,
When it feels like a presence is there.

Not creepy, frightening or horrific,
But a gentle thought,
What if they are here?
With me now.

Beyond a veil which doesn't allow seeing,
Just there watching and being.
That they choose to be close
Is really very flattering.

Not sure how that would work.
Is it an existence whereby
They get to pick the destination?
Or is it, as before, we just like being together.

Suspend

Sitting here dazed,
Not moving, not wanting to.
Sick to my stomach and up to my brain,
Some kind of shift to neutral.

Ahead lies a place I don't want to go.
Confusion, frustration, helplessness
All combine to lock me in place.
There is no choice, it's the direction.

Issues and fractured answers
All piled up on each other.
From which there is nothing
I would want to have around.

The clock ticks every second,
For now, even that is a place
I would rather go, to suspend, a little more
The time that is coming.

The Wave

Are you the messenger or the problem?
Seems to me both.
I don't like what you have to say,
It's erupted in me things best left dormant.

I can't face this.
Like a wave that drives me into the sand,
Powerful, hard to push back
Or get a change in direction.

Leave me be, don't push on me.
You don't know, it's me who lives in this place,
That I don't feel I can face.
It won't go, it never does.

Still, there is an inkling of thinking,
Possibly yet again, this storm-ravaged ship,
Needs to turn the bow,
Straight into the wind.

Elusive and Fleeting

When my heart cracks open,
It floods to the ages.
Ceaseless, floating, searching
For anything solid to connect to.

Somewhere, sometime there must be,
A place to go to gather me.
I only know how to let go,
In the going is a flow reaching.

The push, the challenge, the hurt,
Hurl me through space.
Black, endless and surrounding
Where is the light, the warmth?

Elusive and fleeting,
This journeys end can't be seen.
Another beginning will come,
There are no charts to follow.

The Ledge

Where I am now,
Feels as if, I'm scaling a great mountain cliff.
Scary, intense, every step and handhold unknown.
Then finding a sizeable ledge with a usable cave at
     the rear.

Not much really,
However, the relief borders on immense.
Rest can happen.
Just now, the situation is less intense.

Best I could hope for before,
Was to pitch my tent
On the side of the cliff,
And just be there hanging.

Don't know how long this break will last
Or how difficult the ascent ahead.
At this point, there is no other considering,
Except to appreciate the here and now.

Going with Them

Feeling sick and disconnected,
Watching leaves falling from trees.
Rain softly hits numerous puddles,
Fall is looking for winter.

It's a dark grey day,
Not much better inside.
You are mostly sleeping,
Thankfully, peacefully, it could always be worse.

Moving around the room
Straightening, cleaning, throwing out dead flowers.
Looking at all the pictures again,
Having thoughts about them, some new some not.

No one who hasn't done this, could understand
When life takes a loved one out of mainstream
And changes it all,
You go with them.

Common Thread

We've discussed the loss
Of so many things.
Feeling, memories, skills and functions,
Still we look for a common thread.

Maybe we are trying to see
What we would like to so desperately.
We've cried and worried
And been full of concern.

What may be the hardest yet,
It's all been taken from us.
The decision, no longer ours,
Unknown time and events to come.

Please we ask so passionately,
Make this passing as peaceful as can be.
Full well knowing,
It will be what it will be.

Guilt and Sorrow

Guilt and sorrow are not my friends.
They hang around as if invited,
Tangled and caught up.
I want them to leave, get out!

Guilt for what more can be done,
Sorrow for the continual draining of you.
It's like the rain falling all over,
Covering the terrain.

How many more of these days can last?
Is it to be weeks, months, years?
Discussions are always searched
For clues to what is left clinging.

I can continue to do this
If it's taken one day at a time
But go big picture
And I'm left all over the floor.

Heavy Load

I'm just tired and spent.
Irritated, angry about something,
Nothing in particular is driving it.
Yet everything is.

My stomach is churning,
I can't keep doing this.
I'm done, at the end.
Problem is, that's not an option.

I'm sick of worrying,
There seems to be no end.
This will go on and on.
Survival is wearing me thin.

So many times I've had this
Feeling of being flattened by a truck.
I'm pressed thin on the road.
It won't go away, this heavy load.

Marinated

I don't want this life to change.
In so many ways
I don't want to have to move on.
I want to stay marinated in this one.

All the time it took,
All the experiences that crafted it,
All the effort to create and sustain it,
I'm safe here, why would I leave it?

The seasons come and go,
I like the show each brings.
The cycles turning through time,
Summer's breezes, Fall's crunchy leaves,
    Winter's winds, Spring's flowers.

This conflict roars,
Stay and be hopefully what I like now,
Move on, continue in life's flow.
Time most likely will settle this one.

I Can't

There are two words
Which I work hard to eliminate.
I can't, is my seed patch of despair,
Powerful and always at the ready.

Everything that grabs me
And drags me down,
Starts with those two words,
So effective, so complete.

I can't do this anymore,
I can't take one more day,
I can't financially survive,
I can't see the point of any of this.

Yet time after time,
I have found when starting and doing
Something I have labeled I can't,
The doom dissipates and I can . . .
Or I can change direction.

Spaces and Places

I spent the day
Traveling through spaces and places
I would never have known
If I hadn't been with you.

Knowledge you taught me
Came flooding back.
Things forgotten, stitched back together,
You showed me and it became part of us.

Much of it showed the time
We were able to spend together.
I miss it so much,
It's never coming back.

It's what makes it so hard
To try and move forward.
A lot of times, I don't want to,
Thoughts regarding the future can be
    so frightening.

Push It Back

I try to not let it show
But my reality is
Threatening to tear in two.
Both sides not alive.

A world, shapeless and grey,
The struggle within continues.
Why does this cover my soul
And cloud my mind.

I need to punch through,
To push it back.
This thinking is faint but there,
While overwhelmed it seems so far.

Is this coming down to a choice?
It doesn't feel like there is one.
A mountain of pressure and circumstance
Pushing me down, the only way left,
Is to choose up and fight.

Lost Connection

Where does the feeling of connection go?
I'm lost without it.
Loneliness is hard to avoid,
There are times the connective feeling, felt it
    would never leave.

Now it feels there is no way
It could ever be put back together.
The caring and sharing, the laughter and tears
And everything else in between.

Everything was fine,
Then it wasn't.
How long does this go?
Nothing feels right or comfortable.

It's time to move on.
What if this happens again?
Maybe it won't, maybe it will,
Don't avoid it, if and when it comes.

Direction

I feel for the first time
The line has been crossed,
Between my life as it's known
More into what is to come.

I don't want to leave the comforts
Of all that is around me.
To be orphaned and forced to face
Where to go and what to do.

Time is moving forward,
Change never ceases to happen.
Even if I declare I'm staying the same
Nothing around me will.

Two gifts for me to grasp,
First, the great good gift this life has been,
Second, the open choice to chart a direction.
May the spirit within guide me well.

Invitation

All were gathered for the holidays.
They mostly went as planned,
Except for the invitation made to one of us,
Issued from the other side of this life's veil.

It was discussed and thought over,
In the end it was graciously declined.
Seems the offer was very close,
But the answer was not yet.

There are many different types of things
That hold us in a place.
Some of which,
We are deeply committed to.

Soon, I will lose my biggest one.
A better place for one,
A drifting place for another.
Neither can see what will be.

So Near

As I look back
Sifting through memories
From long ago
A connection of pain is inescapable.

The collective gathering over time
Of one disappointment after another.
Patterns repeating themselves,
What was most sought, elusive?

Yet so many times,
Exactly what was wanted
Was so near, so close.
Why couldn't it have gone a different way?

It's as if a barrier existed,
Like a gate not allowing passage.
Deep reflection and much thought
Has brought me to see, all the things
    that went right.

Other Side

I felt it with surety,
A gift from the other side,
Maybe from the one about to transition.
Whatever the source, I'm grateful.

Peace, calm, contentment, joyful smiles
Combine with a powerful feeling of good energy,
Stories of places beyond,
Where everything is better and I really like it.

Eyes shining with light
Told these stories.
The same ones that were normally sleepy
For multiple days in a row.

Just to be there at that point,
Made me feel better and lighter
Than I had felt in years. It was fleeting
    and fantastic.
Will there be more?

Burning Stress

The time that has passed
Has been for so very long.
Burning stress consumes reality
For days and weeks on end.

It happens over and over,
Suddenly it comes to mind,
Where have I been?
How did all this stack up?

Once again it begins,
Errands, bills, household chores,
   daily living demands,
Connections to others,
Those in the world of the living.

It starts anew,
Like a power outage fixed and coming back on,
What is the true cost of this?
How affected have I been?

Where to Go

I didn't know where to go
Or how to get there.
It seemed as if there was some place
Where I could thrive and it would define me.

The places I looked
Weren't it.
Confusion, stumbling, wanting to know,
I couldn't put it together.

At times it seemed so close,
Then again slipped away,
Leaving me in absolute agony.
Why can't I see this?

What do I have to do?
To put myself in position
For tapping into what I know is there,
To feel, know and live.

Life Is Short

Summer has gone.
Leaves fluttered in the breeze,
The warmth and dryness
Came to beguile us.

So fall came.
And now who is to blame,
For days gone by
That should have had more.

For try as you may,
Time cannot be caught,
Nor is it known
How much you have.

But tomorrow is fresh,
It doesn't have to have
Stains from the past.

Endless Ocean

I need to go to the sea.
In my mind as I visualize,
I can see the endless ocean
And different coastal plains.

Where my thoughts and soul wander,
The salty air fills my nostrils,
The seagulls cry their cries,
The wind is fresh and crisp.

The waves fill my ears
With their beautiful and endless sounds.
When the sun is shining,
The beauty is magnified.

Commitments have kept me from it
But someday I will again explore,
The bays and beaches and tide pools,
To let my being dissolve, in all that surrounds me.

Song Cycle

Strange to think of time,
As in a song,
When the artist first sings it,
Then after they have left this life.

The song stays the same
And always will.
The artist lived their life
Now is gone.

What's created comes into existence,
Then becomes cherished, shared and held onto,
Or is ignored, forgotten and lost,
It could be both, alternating through time.

Our life came to be,
Being an extension of time.
It could be the one or it could be the other,
Where do you want to be?

Eternal Struggle

When here in these times
Of musing and wondering,
As everything set in pattern has been released,
I am again in search of direction.

To commit and follow
Is the chance again.
What though, is the eternal struggle,
Years and years of filtering and experience.

Many paths now known
Not to follow.
Others open and tempt.
Some feel right, some illusionary.

The struggle gets greater
As options are weighed.
An unwelcome and powerful feeling
Surrounds and threatens, fear.

Special in You

How do you hold on
To what is special and right,
When it's not possible to store it all?
Yet when you come across it,

The feelings are fired anew.
Showing how much it means to you
And has so much to do
With who are you.

Daily worries and life's big trials
Work to hammer much of this
Right out of our existence.
Those who can keep it focused

Truly know what blessed is.
Create the time, spend the time,
Make the time,
Don't let the special in you slip your grasp.

A Break

Things don't have to turn out badly
Even though you may feel so.
It's not easy to get out
In front of that.

If your life feels stalled
And every direction you look
Seems a worse place.
Give yourself a break.

Pull back, stop bearing down so hard,
Circumstances matter but so do you.
If you have no idea what sounds fun,
It's long past time to get some.

You can lose yourself to pain and strife,
Probably no one would blame you.
Two things to consider,
This is for you and it's your life.

How It Feels

So this is how it feels,
Now that it's close to the end.
Sleep is breaking the connection
Between here and there.

Peacefulness is winning the fight.
Talking doesn't much matter.
Touch and presence replace it,
It has become the order of the day.

Sitting here so firmly on this side,
It seems I should be able to rouse you
And then we jump into any number of
    conversations,
Now they are no longer there for you.

Sometimes a rustle in bed,
Once in a while a smile,
Sometimes, a surprised look and comment,
Oh, you're still here,
Yes I am.

What to Do

The noise machine is set to songbirds,
They remind me of a place in Hawaii
That I've visited
And hope to see again.

As your days will soon have an end
At some point mine will begin again.
That path can't be seen yet,
Where to go, what to do?

It seems so daunting and scary,
I will be alone.
Something I haven't been in decades,
The possibilities are all different.

As much as I would like to think
That I have a choice in the matter,
The one thing I do know,
Life and change never stop moving on.

A Different Place

You helped me
To a different place,
Beyond where I could ever go
On my own and alone.

Doesn't mean it was all smoothness and light.
Overall though, priceless is the right word.
Extensions of life unlocked and opened up,
I would never give back or redo.

The life mystery of why am I here
Seemed to get filled out,
While not completely finished,
That part needed to be there.

I will never forget you
And who knows when I may join you,
No one has the schedule of time left.
What to put in it?

About the Author

GENE ZIMMERMAN had a thirty-year business career
in various sales and sales management positions within the
consumer electronics, home video, and financial industries
before his wife, Claire, was diagnosed with a tumor in her
spinal cord. For nearly five years, Claire fought coura-
geously as Gene became her caregiver and then, when her
illness demanded full-time professional care, he became
her constant companion, supporter, and advocate.

It was during this time of love and struggle that Gene
was strongly moved to write poetry. Since Claire's death,
Gene has continued to study, take classes, and write poetry.
He lives in Portland, Oregon, and is the proud father of
two grown children, Chloe and Eric.

—

The author realizes that no book is a one-person project,
and considers himself fortunate to have had the assistance
of a team of professionals, along with multiple friends
and family, who have helped make this book possible. The
author would like to acknowledge and thank Jeff Miller
for his invaluable advice and guidance throughout the
entire process, as well as the book's designers, Dan and
Jim at Pratt Brothers Composition, for their creative and
skillful contributions.

Made in the USA
Coppell, TX
10 June 2021